444 WAYS TO SAY
"I Love You"

◆ ◆ ◆

LOVE-IN-ACTION IDEAS FOR HUSBANDS AND WIVES

H. NORMAN WRIGHT

TESTAMENT BOOKS
NEW YORK

This 2002 edition is published by Testament Books, an imprint of Random House Value Publishing, a division of Random House, Inc., New York, by arrangement with Servant Publications.

Random House
New York • Toronto • London • Sydney • Auckland
www.randomhouse.com

Printed in China

A catalog record for this title is available from the Library of Congress.

ISBN: 0-517-22244-2

9 8 7 6 5 4 3 2 1

444 WAYS TO SAY
"I Love You"

◆ ◆ ◆

LOVE-IN-ACTION IDEAS
FOR HUSBANDS

1

Take on the roles of both student and teacher in
your marriage. A fulfilled marriage is one in which
husband and wife teach one another and
learn from one another.

2

Don't compete with your wife—be her friend.
Wish her the best and be enthusiastic about
her achievements. Brag about her!

3

Pray together often. "It is only when a husband and wife pray together before God that they find the secret of true harmony, that the difference in their tastes enriches their home instead of endangering it."[1]

4

It's not your job to "reform" your wife. Encourage
her, praise her, resolve to never take her for
granted, and leave the work of transformation
up to the Holy Spirit.

5
Remember: There is no perfect wife,
perfect husband, or perfect marriage.

6
Silence is not always golden, especially between
husband and wife. Ask your wife when she'd
like to set aside time just to talk.

7
Disagreeing with your wife is one thing; behaving
disagreeably is another. Tell her that you love
her even if you don't see eye to eye.

8
Ask your wife what three words she'd like you to
drop from your vocabulary—then do it!

9
Flowers are never a substitute for the words
"I love you and I want to hear what
you have to say." Give both!

10
Find a recording of your wife's favorite romantic song
and play it for her. Ask her what sounds she finds most
soothing and romantic and provide them for her.

11
Realize that sometimes your love for your wife will be a decision instead of a strong feeling. That's mature, lasting love. That's *agape* love.

12
Fantasizing in marriage is healthy as long as a husband's mind is filled with visions of his wife. Fantasize about your wife!

13
Are you predictable? Do you always follow the
same routine? Make something new happen
in your relationship with your wife today.
Go ahead—surprise her!

14

When you love your wife, you take her feelings and
viewpoints seriously even when they differ from
your own. When you disagree, tell her,
"I see things differently, but maybe I
can learn from you." Believe it!

15

A baseball team doesn't stop working after winning
one game. Winning a woman to be your wife doesn't
mean you stop winning her after marriage.

16

Lectures belong in the classroom, not in the home.
Sacrificial love doesn't demand; it respectfully asks.

17
Genuine love for your wife is incompatible with jealousy, envy, or bitterness. Those responses will push her away rather than draw her close to you.

18
Recognize that expressing your anger is not necessarily bad; it's *how* you express your anger that makes the difference.

19
Does your wife feel nourished and built up during the time you spend at home? Ask her!

20
Ask your wife, "What do you want to be doing five years from now? Ten years from now? How can I help you achieve that?"

21

Settle issues in your marriage as soon as they come up.
"Harmony in marriage exists when there is an
absence of unsettled issues and offenses
between the two of you."[2]

22
Blame in a marriage may identify responsibility, but it does nothing to bring about reconciliation.

23
Fault-finding deeply wounds a wife. Sincere praise, the words "thank you," and nonsexual touches nurture her.

24

Tell your wife how much you value her. "A wife of noble character, who can find? She is worth far more than rubies. Her husband has full confidence in her and lacks nothing of value" (Proverbs 31:10-11 NIV).

25

Don't stop at complimenting your wife once. Look
for something else nice to tell her. She needs
at least one compliment a day!

26

Work at understanding your wife. When she feels
understood, she will feel secure in your love
and respond to you in kind.

27

Be willing to do some things the way your wife does
them. Put the dishes in the cupboard her way or fold
her socks the way she does, just to please her.

28

Keep in mind the reasons you work at your job or career.
"It is not what a man does that determines whether his
work is sacred or secular, it is why he does it."[3]

29

Intimacy in marriage is both sexual and emotional, but
emotional intimacy is the prelude to sexual intimacy.
Your wife needs conversation and attention every day.

30
Nurture friendships with men. Medical research tells
us that men who have close friends enjoy life more and
live longer. List the close friends in your life and tell
them how much you appreciate them.

31
Being a friend to your wife means sharing with her the conversations you have in your mind.

32
For your next anniversary, give your wife a card listing as many reasons why you're glad you married her as years you've been married.

33
According to fishing guides in Alaska, why do women catch more fish than men? Because they listen and follow the guide's instructions better. Hmmmmm....

34
Give your wife a day-by-day calendar with a personal message of love written on the first and fifteenth of each month.

35

In the midst of personal or family crisis, don't waste energy trying to figure out *why*. Trust God, use your energy creatively, and know that solutions will follow.

36

What is God's plan for you and your family at this
time? "The will of God grows on you. That which is
not of God will die—you will lose interest. But the
plan of God will never die."[4]

37
Temptation is inevitable, but it's not the problem.
What you *do* with temptation *can* be the problem.
Will you play with it, entertain it, or evict it?

38
Memorize a Bible verse with your wife every
two weeks. Learn to say with the poet, "I delight
in your decrees; I will not neglect your word"
(Psalm 119:16 NIV).

39
Talk with your wife about how you see God, who He
is, and what He is like. Ask for her viewpoint.

40
Use your competitive spirit to see if you can
"out-serve" your wife. Now there's a goal worth
striving for! Think of three new ways you
can serve your wife this week.

41

Know that you will make mistakes as a husband. Your
wife knows it, and God does, too. Don't give up—
learn from your mistakes and move on.

42

Be conscious of your prayer requests. Are your
prayers compatible with the character of God or
would He violate His nature by giving
you what you're asking for?[5]

43

Does your wife know you well enough to write your biography from age one to fifteen? If not, help her out. She'll love the time you spend together talking.

44

The best way to tell your wife about something you
don't like is to tell her about something you *do* like.
For example: "I really like it when you try
out new recipes on me."

45

Treating your wife in loving ways is like putting money
in a savings account. It pays interest.
Make plenty of deposits!

46

Before making love with your wife some evening,
read aloud from the Song of Solomon.

47

What dreams do you have for your marriage that are
still unrealized? Share them with your wife
and watch them unfold.

48

What cripples a marriage is not the problems and
conflicts, but emotional malnutrition brought
on by apathy and indifference.

49

The words "If only…" stop action and create worry
and a sense of uneasiness for both you and your wife.
When you feel an "If only" coming on, say instead,
"Let's commit this to the Lord."

50
The next time you find yourself arguing with your wife, ask yourself, "Is my goal to punish and dominate my wife, or to understand her?" If needed, redirect your arguments toward the goal of reconciliation.

51

What gift would your wife never expect from you?
Don't ask her. Figure it out for yourself, then give it.
Watch a new image of you develop in her
heart and mind.

52

Differences between you and your wife can either drive you apart and weaken your marriage, or they can help you develop a strength you would never experience any other way. List three ways you and your wife are different and consider how each difference might strengthen your marriage.

53

It's been suggested that a woman's basic needs in
marriage are affection, conversation, honesty and
openness, financial support, and family commitment.[6]
Are your wife's basic needs being met?

54

When your wife lets you know you've hurt or offended
her, think about your goal and choose your response.
Will you be defensive? Resentful? Humble? Sorrowful?
If your goal is to be close again, the choice is clear.

55

For women, emotional loving comes before physical
loving. A wife likes affection even when it has nothing
to do with sex. But nonsexual affection
can lead to great sex!

56

Think about spending the extra time you put into
work with your family instead. You may not
accumulate as many things, but investing
in lives pays great dividends.

57
Purchase a dozen Valentine's cards in February and
send one to your wife each month of the year.

58
When your wife is upset, exhausted, or overwhelmed,
do you know what she needs most of all? Usually it's
simple companionship. She doesn't want to feel alone.
Be there for her. Your presence, patience,
and prayers will help her feel loved.

59
When you have an important decision to make, first
pray for wisdom, then ask your wife for her input.
Keep in mind that she may know best!

60
Don't look at your marital woes through a telephoto
lens, focusing just on the problems. Balance your
perspective. List all the positives about your
marriage and share them with your wife.

61

A wise husband realizes he is incomplete without his wife, and he lets her know how she supports and encourages him.

62

What does your wife do that makes you feel loved, valued, and respected? Write it down, wrap the note around a long stemmed rose, and lay it on her pillow.

63

"If you refuse criticism you will end in poverty
and disgrace; if you accept criticism you are on
the road to fame" (Proverbs 13:18 LB). What
accurate criticism has your wife voiced recently
that you haven't accepted? Admit it to
yourself and to her.

64

Doing things for and with your wife was part of the process of falling in love—and it's how you'll stay in love. Write her a love letter, make her breakfast in bed, clean the house together.

65

Tape-record your conversations with your wife for a
week so you can hear what she hears when you
talk to her. Is your communication helpful,
healing, and sensitive?

66

"If you love someone you will be loyal to him no matter what the cost. You will always believe in him, always expect the best of him, and always stand your ground in defending him"
(1 Corinthians 13:7 LB).

67
"In buying a gift for your wife, practicality can be
more expensive than extravagance."[7]
Go a little wild!

68
You will maintain a close relationship with your wife
only if both of you work to make yourselves
understood. Ask questions, give examples, and
use words and illustrations she can easily relate to.

69

Recognize that the responsibility of the marriage is not yours alone and behave accordingly. Share the responsibility with your wife, and let her know you are sharing it.

70

Pray, study Scripture, or read devotional materials with your wife on a regular basis. The closer a man is to God, the easier it is for him to be open to his wife.

71

Recognize that your wife's happiness is tied up in your own. Don't dwell on the negative in your life; create positive experiences to share with her. Be happy!

72

Listen to your wife. Sit down, stop what you're doing, and really *listen*. It's the only way to find out what's important to her.

73
When your wife asks, "How do I look?" be more
specific than "Fine." How about: "I like the
way you did your hair today," or "The color of
your blouse really makes your eyes sparkle"?

74
Give your wife the same attention you give to a
football game or a basketball game on TV. Sometime
ask her what *she* would prefer watching during the
game. This is sacrificial love!

75

It's far easier to avoid conflict in marriage than to take steps necessary to resolve conflict. Avoidance, however, will only complicate matters. To make conflicts disappear, face them, discuss them, and look for creative ways to resolve them.

76

To what extent are you irresistible to your wife? To what extent are the two of you still incompatible? Are you moving from incompatibility to irresistibility? Think of three ways to reduce your incompatibility, increase your irresistibility, or both.

77
Forgiveness is not a paid-up life insurance policy.
It needs continual investment for a marriage
renewal policy.

78
"A word fitly spoken is like apples of gold in settings of
silver" (Proverbs 25:11 NKJV). The translation
for marriage: "The right word at the right
time, how good it is!"

79
Allow your wife to be unique. Unless a husband has a
death wish, he knows not to say to his wife, "That's
just like a woman!"

80
Sometimes giving your wife a simple hug or holding
her in silence tells her more than words can say.
The right kind of touch says, "I understand.
I accept you the way you are."

81

List the experiences in your marriage so far that
you will want to remember twenty-five years
from now. Ask your wife to create a similar
list and share it with you.

82

Make the following vow to your wife: "Neither by day nor by night will I ever cut you down in company. Not before my family, your family, our family."[8]

83

The quality of your spiritual life will be the remedy for
the aches and pains dispensed by life's stresses. Discuss
your shared spiritual life on a regular basis. Talk about
how you could make it even better.

84

If your lines of communication need repair, be your own handyman. You and your wife may need to tear down some walls before you can rebuild the relationship. Set aside ten minutes every day for uninterrupted talk. It's a beginning.

85
Sex and verbal communication cannot be separated.
One is not a substitute for the other.

86
Keep in mind that love is concern for
what concerns your wife.

87

Remember that in a marriage the question is not so
much who is right, but what is right for the marriage.
Think about it.

88
A loving husband helps his wife discover and develop
her potential. Make a list of your wife's strengths.
Ask her to do the same for you and then share
your lists. Let her know you believe in her.

89
If you are a fast worker, walker, or talker, recognize
that it's easier for you to slow down than for
your wife to speed up. Stay with her!

90
"In marriage, we must cherish the ability to let loose in reckless displays of affection and admiration."[9]

91
Don't suffocate your wife with possessiveness.
Remember that God is the one who owns us;
He has merely entrusted your wife to your care.
Ask her how she would like you to care for her
in new and different ways, then follow through.

92

Invite your wife to a romantic rendezvous by making
a cassette or home videotape. Be creative. Use
background music. She'll love it!

93

Complaining about your wife won't improve your
marriage. Instead, tell her what you like about your
marriage and make positive suggestions that
include action on your part as well as hers.

94

If your wife doesn't hear you when you say "I love you," it may be that you've been saying it the same way for too long. Say it in a way that will surprise her! Write it on the bathroom mirror or call her on the phone and sing it to her.

95
"High blood pressure in marriage is caused by fat clogging the veins of communication."[10]

96
One of the greatest gifts you can give your wife is the right to fail and to be imperfect. After all, it's what *you* want from *her*, isn't it?

97

If you think you've made some positive changes your
wife has requested, evaluate them with *her* measuring
stick as well as your own. Ask her what she thinks.
Don't argue with her answer.

98

"Putting your wife in the Number One slot just below
God doesn't shackle you to the house; instead, it frees
you of the dread of going home."[11]

99
Volunteer to watch the children for an afternoon or
evening and encourage your wife to do
something she would enjoy.

100
A loving husband is as careful with his wife as he is
with his favorite tools, golf clubs, or new car.

101
Have you ever told your wife, "You make me so angry"? Does she really have that much power over you? Is there another possibility? Think about it.

102
Look up I Peter 3:7 to find out every husband's two major responsibilities. Are you doing them?

103

Loving your wife means recognizing specific needs and
offering to meet them. Be sure to meet her needs in
the way she'd like you to. If she needs some time away
from the kids, for instance, does she want to leave
them at home and go out for the evening, or would
she prefer you to take them out so she can get things
done at home? If you're unsure, ask.

104
Listening to your wife means you're not thinking about your response while she's still talking (Proverbs 18:13). When she finishes talking, summarize what she said to make sure you understood.

105
Instead of buying an anniversary card this year, write your own and have it printed on parchment paper.

106
What is your plan for ongoing maintenance and renewal of your marriage? This year, read a marriage enhancement book together or attend a marriage class or seminar. Make the arrangements yourself this time.

107

When a husband and wife talk about their thoughts and feelings with each other, every problem is diminished and every joy expanded. Next time, be the one to initiate this kind of sharing.

108

All husbands offend their wives at some point. Some
are oblivious to their wife's hurt, some ignore it,
and some admit their offense and ask forgiveness.
What has been your pattern? Practice asking
forgiveness. It will draw you closer together.

109
A meaningful sexual experience for your wife
is related directly to your gentleness with her.
Be gentle in word and touch.

110
On a scale of 0 to 10, where would you rate your
marriage today? Where would your wife rate it?
Predict her answer and then (gulp) ask her.

111
There are two women in every marriage—a man's wife and his mother. Your allegiance should be to your wife. Ask her how you're doing on this one.

112
Does the TV in your home build your marriage relationship or detract from it? Ask your wife if she would agree to keep the television off for a month so you can both work on your communication with each other.

113
Change is a vital part of a growing marriage. List three
ways you are different this year compared to last.
Ask your wife what she thinks.

114
Talk with your wife about your budget, bank accounts,
and tax returns. Don't "protect" her from your
financial worries; withholding information can
lead to insecurity and mistrust on her part.

115

Often when a woman is feeling stressed, she moves toward her husband for comfort. Give your wife a listening ear, a gentle hug, and a strong shoulder—and no advice unless she asks for it!

116

Marriage often turns out to be more than you
expected. But you and your wife can shape the
future of your marriage by determining its
direction. List three common goals you and
your wife have for your marriage. If you
don't have any, don't wait any longer!

117

Forgiveness in marriage is tied to grace rather than
justice. It lets your wife off the hook. It doesn't
make her pay again and again for the same failure.
Forgive and forget.

118

When a man loves his wife, he opens himself up to a
new level of hurt. But understand that when a woman
feels unloved by her husband, the pain of her
loneliness is intense. Take the risk. Tell your
wife daily that you love her.

119
If you think of your wife as overly talkative, try thinking of her as expressive and thorough instead. Learn
something new from her attention to detail!

120
Whenever you think, "I should have listened to her,"
let your wife know. Your standing in her
eyes will increase.

121
The marriage relationship is God's way of reflecting his eternal love for his people. What priority should we give to it? What priority do you give to it?

122
Listen for God's voice. "And if you leave God's paths and go astray, you will hear a Voice behind you say, 'No, this way; walk here'" (Isaiah 30:21 LB).

123

Romance in marriage doesn't just happen; it's something you *make* happen by thought, attention, desire, and action.

124

God does not quit on us. A husband's wedding vows to his wife are a reflection of God's pledge to never leave us and never give up on us. What area of your marriage could use more attention and effort?

125
Have you ever thought about what your wife might look like twenty years from now, or what you might look like? Talk with her about your thoughts.

126
Be careful what you say to your wife in anger. Hurt that comes from angry words can last long after you've forgotten what your anger was all about.

127
Make a list of your needs and ask God to show you
which are important. Let Him decide. Better to lead a
God-centered life than a need-centered life.

128
Think about how much time you spend working.
Tell your wife what your work means to you
and what you would like to be doing in your
work ten years from now.

129
Failing doesn't make you a failure in your marriage.
Giving up, withdrawing, viewing yourself as a failure,
and refusing to learn from your experience might!

130

A husband doesn't *have* to serve his wife, care for
her, help her. He *gets* to! Tell your wife you've
learned it's a privilege to love her. Ask how
you can serve her even more.

131

In your marital disagreements, do you take the role of
solution-finder or warrior? Only one role allows both
you and your wife to be winners. Warrior isn't it!

132

Give your wife the best gift of all: your time and attention. One husband gave his wife a box with a note in it for her birthday. The note read, "I will give you 365 hours this year to talk and share with me. An hour a day. The time is yours."

133

Friendship between a husband and wife is rated as the
number one reason for marital happiness. Having a
close friendship comes from being a good friend.
Laughing, playing, talking, and working
together builds friendship.

134

On a scale of 0 to 10, how important are your possessions to you? "Then [Jesus] said to them, 'Watch out! Be on your guard against all kinds of greed; a man's life does not consist in the abundance of his possessions'" (Luke 12:15 NIV).

135
The next time you are sick, notice how you act with
your wife. Are you pleasant or unapproachable?
Are you easy to take care of or should you be
confined to an isolation ward?!

136
Never seek guidance from God about something
He has already forbidden in His Word. All we
need to do is be obedient.

137
"The only time to stop temptation is at the point of
recognition. If one begins to argue and engage
in a hand to hand combat, temptation
almost always wins the day."[12]

138
Men often relate to God in one of four ways: "Give
me," "Use me," "Make me," or "Search me, O God,
and know my heart." Where are you today?

139
Ask your wife how you could be better at loving and
serving her. Be ready to hear her answer.
Thank her for her suggestions.

140
Don't let the sun go down on your anger.
Resolve your differences as soon as possible—
a great idea in marriage.

141
Write your wife a note telling her she's
a memorable person and why.[13]

142
Tell your wife on a regular basis, "I love you more
than yesterday and less than tomorrow."

143
If your wife ever has an auto accident, *don't* ask
"How's the car?" before you ask, "How are you?!"

144
Remind yourself often that husbands who give a little
love find it goes a long way, and husbands who give
a lot of love find it just keeps going and
going and going forever.

145

A 50/50 marriage doesn't work; it's too hard to figure out if you and your wife have both come halfway. With a 100/100 commitment, there isn't a question.

146

Tell your wife how you see God working in your lives. "Unless the Lord builds the house, its builders labor in vain" (Psalm 127:1 NIV).

147
Encourage your wife in specific ways. A woman
who knows her husband supports her will
trust him more and be more open.

148
Romance is like a coal that needs your breath and
patience to ignite. If you want a stronger
marriage, take a few breaths and blow!

149

Your wife has a love bank. Every time you interact with
her you make a deposit or a withdrawal. Have
you checked the ledger lately? Keep those
books balanced![14]

150

When your wife is struggling with a problem, *ask* if
she wants suggestions before giving them. If she
does, give them gently and lovingly. Be aware
of your tone of voice.

151

When a husband gives his wife second place—because
he gives his work, sports, or some other interest first
place—she has three choices. She can accept second
place, press for first place and eventually win, or
press for first place until she loses heart.
Why put her through that?[15]

152

Ask your wife how the way you handle frustration or
express anger makes her feel and how it affects
your marriage. Ask her how you could
express those feelings differently.

153

A great husband is one who can satisfy one woman all
his life long—and who can be satisfied by one woman
all his life long. It takes effort, time, commitment,
and the grace of God, but it's possible. Make
this your goal for the life of your marriage.

154

If your marriage seems dull, perhaps it's you! Maybe
you're stuck in your routine. Maybe you're too
predictable. Shock your wife! Be unusually
creative and totally unpredictable.

155

"Instead of focusing on our mates—how much is lacking—let's look at ourselves and the size of the debt
God has forgiven us. Surely he bears with our failings.
Let us commit to bear with each other's failings
when we are weak and build each other up."[16]

156

Talk with your wife on an ongoing basis about how
both you and she would like your marriage to be
different. Listen without defensiveness. Take
time to think about her ideas and yours,
and come back to the discussion later.

157
A husband and wife who are friends don't attempt to
control or dominate one another. Respect your wife's
intelligence and integrity. Ask often, "What do you
think?" Say often, "Let's try it your way."

158
Begin your day by leaving a note asking your wife how
you could be a better listener. Thank her when she
responds. Try her suggestions!

159

The love-talk that a couple shares before marriage is too often, after marriage, replaced by other kinds of communication. Take time to reflect, then list the things you used to talk about. Ask your wife to do the same. Introduce those topics back into your conversations.

160

Talking may not be everything, but it sure beats
avoiding important issues. Avoidance causes
problems to grow. When you find yourself
avoiding your wife, ask yourself, "What is our
disagreement? How can we resolve it?"

161

Conflict can open as many doors as it closes in a
marriage. When you allow it to open a door between
you and your wife, you'll see your differences
disappear. What are some things you can do
to resolve some of your differences? Think
about it and come up with a list of ideas.

162

Love in marriage says, "Will you forgive me for
the hurt I've caused you?" When have you said this?
Do you need to say it now?

163

When your wife asks forgiveness for an offense against
you, remember that true forgiveness will elevate her
self-esteem, not depress it. When you tell her you
forgive her, always tell her that you love and
value her as well.

164
Before giving your wife advice, ask her if she wants it. She may just need you to listen.

165
When you are silent, does your wife really know what you're thinking? Or do you just think she does? Volunteer what you are thinking rather than waiting to be asked. She'll love you for it.

166

"Sex is a God-ordained means of assuring your partner that she is the most important person in the world right here, right now." Make it creative, romantic, and sensitive to your wife's needs and timing.[17]

167
Lines open to God are invariably open to one another,
for a person cannot be genuinely open to God
and closed to his mate.[18]

168
When you love and support the best in your wife,
many of the things that irritate you either disappear
or don't bother you as much.

169

Go to the library and check out a book of romantic poems. Give one to your wife every day in a hand-written note. Or read one aloud each day with the lights dimmed.

170

When you find yourself arguing with your wife, stop
yourself and listen to her. Then respond with, "If I
understand your position, you are saying…" and
restate what you heard. When you stop to
consider both sides of an issue, you'll be
amazed how marital discord diminishes.

171

When your wife has had a bad day, the best words you can say are, "I believe in you, and so does God. What can I do to make the rest of your day easier?"

172

Make your wife a priority. It's good for you as well as for her. "The more important a woman feels she is to her husband, the more she encourages him to do the activities she knows he enjoys."[19]

173
The purpose for giving your wife a gift is to delight
her. Will a season ticket to the football games, a shot-
gun, or going to a hockey game
really delight her? Ask!

174
You *can* enjoy shopping with your wife! Plan it in
advance as you would a fishing trip.

175

When you walk in the door after work, who or what gets your immediate attention? The mail, the cat, the kids, the TV? Your wife wants to be Number One. Before you do anything else, greet her with affection and genuine interest: "I've missed you," "It's good to see you," "Tell me about your day." Avoid "Where's the mail?" or "What's for dinner?" until your wife knows she's the reason you came home!

176
Who hears about it when your wife upsets you?
Nobody? Your mother? Your friends? Next time, let
her know directly but calmly that you are upset and
what you would like her to do differently.

177
Think of two or three times recently you've shared
with your wife feelings of failure, sadness, or disappointment. If you can't, today's a new day.
Let her see you as you are.

178
Make it your business to know at least five of your
wife's needs and how to meet those needs in a way
she desires. Most women, for example, have a
need for affection. It would be difficult
to give too many hugs, cards, or flowers!

179
If you're too tired to talk, let your wife know.
Be sure to tell her when you think you'll
be ready to talk to her.

180
If your wife tells you she's hurt because you're not talking to her, understand that she may be interpreting your silence as "He doesn't care" or "He doesn't love me." Give her whatever reassurance she needs.

181
Satisfied wives have husbands who ask, "Where would *you* like to go on vacation this year?!"
Why not ask her today?

182
Scripture teaches us to praise God (Psalm 100:4),
others (Ephesians 4:29), and specifically our wives
(Proverbs 31:28). Think of three ways
you've praised your wife recently.

183
Come up with a list of gifts you *think* your wife would
like to receive from you. Show her the list and ask her
opinion. How well did you do? Give her one
of her choices this week.

184

Marriage is the best place to alter bad habits or offensive behaviors. Ask your wife if there's anything you do she would prefer you didn't do.

185

Be patient before God when the road seems long. "But those who wait on the Lord shall renew their strength; they shall mount up with wings like eagles, they shall run and not be weary. They shall walk and not faint" (Isaiah 40:31 NKJV).

186

Love can die when a husband and wife forget how to talk to each other, when they don't make time for romance.[20] Surprise your wife this week with a romantic evening you plan yourself.

187

"May your fountain be blessed, and may you rejoice in the wife of your youth" (Proverbs 5:18 NIV). Think of three reasons you rejoice over the woman you married and give her a special card expressing these.

188

Lead your wife with love. Don't play the part of a general commanding the troops or an animal trainer snapping his whip.

189

Being your wife's friend means encouraging her to reach her potential and delighting in her success as if you had hit a home run in the World Series. Think of a personal goal your wife has recently achieved and plan a celebration with a few close friends.

190

Feeling trapped? When everyone in your life is demanding a piece of you and there isn't enough to go around, slip away for a quiet conversation with someone you know will just listen. How about God?

191

If your work were taken away from you for the next six months (gulp), how would you feel about yourself? Discuss this question with your wife sometime.

192

"A generous man will prosper; he who refreshes others will himself be refreshed" (Proverbs 11:25 NIV). List the ways that you are generous toward your wife. Time? Helping around the house? Money? How else?

193

Would you like to discover the will of God for your marriage? Go before God together. Ask Him what He wants for your marriage and determine to do it!

194
"If we wait until we have resolved every doubt, every question, before following God, we will never do anything with our life. We must step out by faith."[21]

195
Develop an early warning system to combat temptation in your life. Pray together with your wife every day. Memorize 1 Corinthians 10:13 together.

196
How does your wife know that you really care for her?
List three specific ways. If you don't know, ask. Then
ask, "How else would you like to be cared for?"

197

In one of your braver moments, ask your wife for three
things you could improve on. Tell her you respect
her judgment and you'd like her help in
becoming a better husband.

198
Write your wife a note that says, "You just go on getting better every day!"[22] Tape it to the mirror in your bedroom.

199
"When our mates have strengths we should affirm them, but never pressure them to perform. To criticize our mates at the point of their strength is to kill their courage."[23]

200

Many men remember numbers easily: batting averages,
stock market figures, field goal percentages. Do you
know what your wife would like you to remember?
Ask her. Write down specific dates and
occasions and refer to your list!

201
An inexpensive gift that gives a thousand percent
return is an activities calendar with "Family Time"
written on several days of each month.

202
Remember that love isn't an act; it's a way of life. It's
being there during good times and not-so-good times.
Being there is always possible when Jesus is
invited to be there, too.

203

Talk to your wife about her thoughts and concerns about your marriage. Learn to see life through her eyes as well as your own. She may see things you miss.

204

Some husbands fail to contribute to their wife's
happiness, some actively contribute to her
unhappiness, and some make her feel like
the most important woman on earth.
How does your wife feel?

205

Signs that a husband and wife have an intimate relationship: he opens the car door for her; he holds her hand in public; he avoids saying things in front of other people that will embarrass her; he accepts her when she reaches out to him.

How are you doing?

206

Take your wife away for a romantic weekend. Tell her
in advance you will not think or talk about work, you
won't discuss problems, and you won't turn on the
TV. Be her servant for the weekend.

207
Give your wife a back rub. Brush her hair.
Drop by her office in the afternoon.
Call her just to say, "I love you."

208
When your wife wants to talk, turn off or put away
any distractions. Look her in the eye and give her
feedback so she knows you're listening.

209
Leave your wife a note in the morning asking her what it is you do that helps her feel close, warm, protected, and understood. Ask her what else you can do.

210
Reflect on the ways you communicated with your wife in the early days of your courtship. How did two strangers become intimate friends? Think of three ways you communicate with her now that keeps your intimacy alive. If you can't, ask her for feedback.

211
Listen sensitively. Give frequent feedback. Don't
interrupt, especially to say, "Get to the point!"

212
Don't assume you know what your wife is going to say
before she says it. Assumptions lead to distortions, so
listen carefully. She may surprise you!

213
Forgive truly. "Forgiving" your wife only if she promises never to fail again is not forgiveness. True forgiveness trusts and believes in the one you love.

214
Overlook your wife's shortcomings, but never overlook her potential! Let her know you believe in her. Ask how you can help her reach her goals.[24]

215

Tell your wife that she's more important to you than
your work—then find some way to prove it to her!

216

Husbands and wives comfort one another in time of
need. How does your wife like you to comfort her?
Don't guess about this—ask if you don't know. How
do you prefer she comfort you? Tell her.

217

Remember that your wife's sense of timing is different
from your own. If you recover quickly from a quarrel,
wonderful—but don't expect her to be there, too.
Healing can't be rushed. Give her time.

218

Teach your wife gently. Use positive modeling,
gentle prodding, encouraging words. Let her
know you believe in her.

219

Be teachable. Listen to your wife, learn from her
positive modeling, accept her gentle prodding.
She believes in you!

220

If you haven't already, you will experience the death of
a parent, a close friend, a child, or your spouse. Now is
the time to think about how you will handle it.
Discuss it with your wife.

221

Working out a disagreement with your wife?
Attack the problem rather than the person.
Suggest alternatives rather than stubbornly
sticking to your solution as though
it were the only one.

222

"Marriage is not so much finding the right person as it is *being* the right person."[25] Are you the husband you wanted to be when you married? If not, it's still possible to become that man.

NOTES

1. Paul Tournier, *The Healing of Persons* (New York: Harper and Row, 1965), 88-89.
2. Gary Smalley, *If Only He Knew* (Grand Rapids, Mich.: Zondervan, 1979), 75, adapted.
3. A.W. Tozer, *The Pursuit of God* (Harrisburg, Penn.: Christian Publications, 1948), 127.
4. David Wilkerson, *I'm Not Mad at God* (Minneapolis: Bethany, 1967), 32.
5. Richard Exley, *The Making of a Man* (Tulsa: Honor, 1993), 173, adapted.
6. Willard F. Harley, Jr., *His Needs, Her Needs* (Grand Rapids, Mich.: Revell, 1986), 13.
7. Max Lucado, *When God Whispers Your Name* (Dallas: Word, 1994), 43.
8. Charlie Shedd, *Letters to Philip* (Old Tappan, N.J.: Revell, 1968), 64.
9. James R. Bjorge, *Forty Ways to Say I Love You* (Minneapolis: Augsburg, 1978), 24.
10. Bjorge, 59-60.
11. Smalley, 46.
12. Thomas à Kempis.
13. Shedd, 31.
14. Harley, 19, adapted.
15. Patrick M. Morley, *Two Part Harmony* (Nashville: Nelson, 1994), 79, adapted.
16. Morley, 143.

17. Charlie Shedd, *Letters to Karen* (Nashville: Abingdon, 1965), 111.

18. Dwight Small, *After You Say I Do* (Grand Rapids, Mich.: Revell, 1968), 214.

19. Smalley, 47.

20. James Dobson, *Dr. Dobson Answers Your Questions* (Wheaton, Ill.: Tyndale, 1982), 329.

21. Exley, 141.

22. Shedd, *Letters to Philip*, 33.

23. Morley, 143.

24. Bjorge, 30, adapted.

25. Shedd, *Letters to Karen*, 13.

444 WAYS TO SAY
"I Love You"
• • •

LOVE-IN-ACTION IDEAS FOR
HUSBANDS AND WIVES

H. NORMAN WRIGHT

TESTAMENT BOOKS
NEW YORK

444 WAYS TO SAY
"I Love You"

• • •

LOVE-IN-ACTION IDEAS
FOR WIVES

1

Build your husband's self-confidence and motivate
him to action by letting him know you
need him and appreciate him.

2

Men tend to take things literally. When you ask your
husband to do something for you, phrase it with a
"Would you?" instead of a "Could you?"
He'll know you want help and aren't
just asking a hypothetical question![1]

3
What's your husband's favorite hobby? Study up
on the topic through reading, lessons, or
whatever it takes, and one day surprise
him with your knowledge and skill!

4
If your husband becomes quiet during a discussion,
don't assume he's ignoring you. Many men like to
put important issues on the back burner and think
about them before talking. Give him time.

5

When you share your feelings with your husband, let
him know you're not trying to tell him what to do—
you just want him to listen and consider how you feel.
Tell him directly, "When you listen to my
feelings I feel loved and supported."

6

Trust your husband. He needs to know you believe he
wants the best for you and he is doing his best in the
marriage. When you are open and receptive to
what he has to offer, you fulfill his need
for love. In turn, he loves back.[2]

7
Write down your husband's requests so you can
remember them without having to be reminded.
He'll notice!

8
Let your husband know ahead of time what kind of
support you want from him. You'll find it easier
to share your concerns and feelings when *you*
know *he* knows what to expect.[3]

9

Take a few minutes to freshen up and fix your face and
hair before your husband comes home from work.
He'll know you did it just for him.

10

Many men remember numbers easily: batting averages,
stock market figures, field goal percentages. Does
your husband know what you'd like him
to remember? Write down specific dates
and occasions for him as reminders.

11
Many men don't want to be bothered when they're upset or in a bad mood. Ask, "Is there something I can do to help, or would you prefer I leave you alone? I'm willing to do either."

12
When your husband asks forgiveness for an offense, let him know that you love and value as well as forgive him. True forgiveness does not depress one's self-esteem; it elevates it.

13

Reconciliation makes equals of a husband and wife.
In true reconciliation, neither is put down. Do you feel
equal in your relationship? Does your husband feel
as though you value his contributions? Ask!

14

Be direct with requests. Not: "It would really be nice to eat out one night this week," delivered with a sigh. Instead, simply: "Would you take me out to dinner one night this week?"

15

Romance in marriage doesn't just happen. You can make it happen by your attention, desire, thoughts, and actions.

16

When was the last time you gave your husband a back
rub? Fixed his favorite dessert? Dropped by his office
in the afternoon? Called to say, "I love you and
I'm looking forward to seeing you tonight"?
Surprise him!

17

Ask your husband what two or three prayer requests
he would like to have answered in the next thirty days.
Write the requests on cards, leaving space to write in
answers, and place them where you'll both see
them every day. Rejoice with him when
his prayers are answered!

18

Praise your husband in front of others. Tuck special
notes in his shirt pocket or briefcase. A man is
much more open to change when he feels
loved, trusted, and accepted.

19

What does your husband do that makes you feel loved,
valued, and respected? Write it down and slip it into
a recent issue of his favorite magazine or tape it
to the sports page of the newspaper.

20
Your husband welcomes soothing, helpful, brief, and
sensitive communication. Ask him what time of
day is best for him to talk with you, too.

21
Pay attention when your husband talks to you. Turn
off or put away any distractions. Look him in
the eye and give him feedback. An inexpensive
but extremely valuable gift!

22

Admire your husband. Give him thanks, approval, and appreciation. He'll feel secure in your admiration and want to continue to meet your needs.

23

If your husband doesn't hear you when you say "I love you," it may be that you've been saying it the same way for too long. Say it in a way that will surprise him! Write it on the bathroom mirror or in his daily calendar, or clip a note to the sun visor in his car.

24

It's not your job to reform your husband. Encourage
him, praise him, never take him for granted.
You can request change, but leave the work
of transformation up to the Holy Spirit.

25

Don't compete with your husband—be his friend.
Wish him the best and be enthusiastic about his
achievements. Brag about him!

26

Take on the roles of both student and teacher in your
marriage. A fulfilled marriage is one in which
husband and wife teach one another and
learn from one another.

27

Pray together often. "It is only when a husband and wife pray together before God that they find the secret of true harmony, that the difference in their tastes enriches their home instead of endangering it."[4]

28

Talk with your husband about your budget, bank accounts, and tax returns. Withholding your worries and concerns about finances only makes them greater.

29
Remember: There is no perfect husband,
perfect wife, or perfect marriage.

30
Genuine love for your husband is incompatible with
jealousy, envy, or bitterness. Those responses will push
him away rather than draw him close to you.

31
Silence is not always golden, especially between
husband and wife. Ask your husband if he'd
like to set aside time just to talk.

32
Disagreeing with your husband is one thing; behaving
disagreeably is another. Tell him that you love
him even if you don't see eye to eye.

33
Find a recording of your husband's favorite song and play it for him. Ask him what sounds he finds most soothing and relaxing and provide them for him.

34
Realize that sometimes your love for your husband will be a decision instead of a strong feeling. That's mature, lasting love. That's *agape* love.

35

When your husband is upset, exhausted, or
overwhelmed, do you know what he needs
most of all? It may be simple companionship.
It may be space, or peace and quiet. Be there
for him. Your sensitivity, presence,
patience, and prayers will
help him feel loved.

36
Fantasizing in marriage is healthy as long as a wife's
mind is filled with visions of her husband.
Fantasize about your husband!

37
When you love your husband, you take his feelings and
viewpoints seriously even when they differ
from your own. When you disagree, tell him,
"I see things differently, but maybe I can
learn from you." Believe it!

38

Telling your husband, "You don't understand" won't help him understand your needs better. That phrase is accusative and he won't hear it. Try, "Let me say it another way."[5]

39

Never seek guidance from God about something He has already forbidden in His Word. All we need to do is be obedient.

40
Lectures belong in the classroom, not in the home.
Sacrificial love doesn't demand; it respectfully asks.

41
Ask once; don't nag. If your husband complains,
don't argue. Let him make his own decision
in his own time.

42
Settle issues in your marriage as soon as they come up.
"Harmony in marriage exists when there is an
absence of unsettled issues and offenses
between the two of you."[6]

43
Blame in a marriage may identify responsibility, but it
does nothing to bring about reconciliation.

44

Limit your discussion of problems to one issue at a
time. Let your husband know that listening to you
may be the best part of the solution.

45

Recognize that expressing your anger is not
necessarily bad; it's *how* you express your
anger that makes the difference.

46

Intimacy in marriage is both sexual and emotional,
but emotional intimacy is the prelude to sexual
intimacy. Let your husband know that when he
gives you conversation and attention every day
of your marriage, you are able to respond to
him sexually to a greater degree.

47

For your next anniversary, give your husband a card
listing as many reasons why you're glad you
married him as years you've been married.

48

Many men resist shopping. Make it interesting for
your husband by presenting him with a map of your
favorite mall, and a list of items that would interest
him, along with a list of the stores in which
he'll find each item. He'll love it!

49

In the midst of personal or family crisis, don't waste energy trying to figure out *why*. Trust God, use your energy creatively, and know that solutions will follow.

50

What is God's plan for you and your family at this time? "The will of God grows on you. That which is not of God will die—you will lose interest. But the plan of God will never die."[7]

51
Temptation is inevitable, but it's not the problem.
What you *do* with temptation *can* be the problem. Will
you play with it, entertain it, or evict it?

52
Talk with your husband about how you see God, who
He is, and what He is like. Ask about his viewpoint.

53
What cripples a marriage is not the problems and
conflicts, but emotional malnutrition brought
on by apathy and indifference.

54
See if you can "out-serve" your husband. Now there's a worthy competition! Think of three new ways you can serve your husband this week.

55
Know that you will make mistakes as a wife. Your husband knows it, and God does, too. Don't give up—learn from your mistakes and move on.

56

It was through the process of doing things for and with your husband that you fell in love. It's how you'll stay in love. Send the kids out to a baby-sitter, have a bubble bath waiting for your husband when he gets home, share a picnic dinner in front of the fireplace. Be wild and creative!

57

Do whatever you can to help your husband feel
accepted. A husband who feels secure in his
role responds to his wife with love.

58

Does your husband know you well enough to write
your biography from age one to fifteen? If not, help
him out. You'll generate a great discussion, and
he'll understand you better.

59

Treating your husband in loving ways is like putting money in a savings account. It pays interest. Make plenty of deposits!

60

When your husband lets you know you've hurt or offended him, think about your goal and choose your response. Will you be defensive? Resentful? Humble? Sorrowful? If your goal is to be close again, the choice is clear.

61
Before making love with your husband some evening,
read aloud from the Song of Solomon.

62
What dreams do you have for your marriage that are
still unrealized? Share them with your husband and
create an opportunity for them to unfold.

63

What three questions or phrases would your husband
like you to drop from your vocabulary? If you
don't know, ask. Then do it!

64

The words "If only..." stop action and create
unnecessary worry and a sense of uneasiness in
your marriage. When you feel an "If only"
coming on, say instead, "Let's commit
this to the Lord."

65

What gift would your husband never expect from you?
Don't ask him. Figure it out for yourself, then
give it. Watch a new image of you develop
in his heart and mind.

66
Before giving your husband advice, ask if he wants it.
He may just need you to accept his words in silence.

67
Allow your husband to be unique. "That's just like a
man!" or "You men are all the same!" does nothing to
promote understanding.

68

Differences between you and your husband can either
drive you apart and weaken your marriage, or they can
help you develop a strength you would never
experience any other way. List three ways you
and your husband are different and consider
how each difference might strengthen
your marriage.

69

Help your husband think about and fulfill his potential. Ask him, "What do you want to be doing five years from now? Ten years from now? How can I help you achieve those things?"

70

Working out a disagreement with your husband? Attack the problem rather than the person. Suggest alternatives rather than stubbornly sticking to your solution as though it's the only one.

71

Be willing to do some things the way your husband does them. Organize the tools in the garage his way, or put the mail next to his chair instead of on the kitchen table, just to please him.

72

Purchase a dozen Valentine's Day cards in February and send one to your husband each month of the year.

73

When you have an important decision to make, first
pray for wisdom, then ask your husband for his input.
Keep in mind that he may know best!

74

"If you refuse criticism you will end in poverty and disgrace; if you accept criticism you are on the road to fame" (Proverbs 13:18 LB). What accurate criticism has your husband voiced recently that you haven't accepted? Admit it to yourself and to him.

75

"If you love someone you will be loyal to him no
matter what the cost. You will always believe
in him, always expect the best of him, and
always stand your ground in defending him"
(1 Corinthians 13:7 LB).

76
Don't look at your marital woes through a telephoto lens, focusing just on the problems. Balance your perspective. List all the positives about your marriage and share them with your husband.

77

Pray, study Scripture, or read devotional materials
with your husband on a regular basis. The closer
you are to God, the easier it will be for you
to be open to your husband.

78

Don't assume you know what your husband is think-
ing when he's silent. Tell him, "There's no way
I can know what you're thinking right now, but
I'd like to know. I promise if you decide to
share with me I'll just listen without comment."
Then keep your part of the bargain!

79

Leave a note on the dashboard of your husband's car
asking how you could be a better listener. Thank him
for his suggestions and put them into practice.

80

It's far easier to avoid conflict in marriage than to take
steps necessary to resolve conflict. Avoidance,
however, will only complicate matters. To make
conflicts disappear, face them, discuss them,
and look for creative ways to resolve them.

81

To what extent are you irresistible to your husband?
To what extent are the two of you still incompatible?
Are you moving from incompatibility to irresistibility?
Think of three ways to reduce your incompatibility,
increase your irresistibility, or both.

82
Forgiveness is not a paid-up life insurance policy.
It needs continual investment for
a marriage renewal policy.

83

Frustrated when your husband doesn't talk to you?
Practice patience and acknowledge his efforts at
communication. Express appreciation when he
listens to you, listen without interruption
when he does talk, and don't pressure him
for more. Eventually he'll share more with you.

84

"A word fitly spoken is like apples of gold in settings of silver" (Proverbs 25:11 NKJV). The translation for marriage: "The right word at the right time, how good it is!" When is the right time for you to talk to your husband?

85

List the experiences in your marriage so far that you
will want to remember twenty-five years from
now. Ask your husband to create a similar
list and share it with you.

86

Make the following vow to your husband: "Neither by
day nor by night will I ever cut you down in company.
Not before my family, your family, our family."[8]

87

The quality of your spiritual life will be the remedy for
the aches and pains dispensed by life's stresses. Discuss
your shared spiritual life on a regular basis. Talk about
how you could make it even better.

88

If your lines of communication need repair, be your
own handyman. You and your husband may need to
tear down some walls before you can rebuild the relationship. Set aside ten minutes every day for
uninterrupted talk. It's a beginning.

89

Remember that in a marriage the question is not so much who is right, but what is right for the marriage. Think about it.

90

A loving wife calls her husband's strengths to his attention and helps him discover and develop his potential. Make a list of your husband's strengths. Ask him to do the same for you and then share your lists. Let him know you believe in him.

91
Work hard at making yourself understood. Ask questions, give examples, repeat your responses, use words and illustrations your husband can identify with. Focus on visual examples.

92
Invite your husband to a romantic rendezvous by making a cassette or home video tape. Have fun with it! Play it for him in a private moment. He'll appreciate your creativity!

93

"I delight in your decrees; I will not neglect your word" (Psalm 119:16 NIV). Do you have a regular pattern for memorizing scripture? If not, suggest to your husband that you memorize a verse together every two weeks.

94

"High blood pressure in marriage is caused by fat clogging the veins of communication."[9]

95
Are you predictable? Do you always follow the same
routine? Make something new happen in your
relationship with your husband today.
Go ahead—surprise him!

96

Stress tends to make men quiet, withdrawn, or irritable. Avoid giving your husband advice when he's feeling stressed; instead, offer him space, a listening ear, a gentle hug, or the reassurance of lovemaking.

97
In marriage, we must cherish the ability to let loose in reckless displays of affection and admiration.[10]

98
One of the greatest gifts you can give your husband is the right to fail and to be imperfect. After all, it's what *you* want from *him*, isn't it?

99

If you think you've made some positive changes your husband has requested, evaluate them with *his* measuring stick as well as your own. Ask him what he thinks. Don't argue with his answer.

100

Have you ever told your husband, "You make me so angry"? Does he really have that much power over you? Is there another possibility? Think about it.

101
Loving your husband means recognizing specific needs
and offering to meet them. Be sure to meet his needs
in the way he'd like you to. If you're unsure, ask.

102
Instead of complaining to others about your marriage,
tell your husband what you *do* like about your
marriage and make positive suggestions for
making it even better.

103

Listening to your husband means you're not thinking about your response while he's still talking (Proverbs 18:13). When he finishes talking, summarize what he said to make sure you understood.

104

Instead of buying an anniversary card this year, write
your own and have it printed on parchment paper.
Have it delivered to your husband in an unusual way: a
business associate, a neighbor, the family dog!

105

What is your plan for ongoing maintenance and
renewal of your marriage? This year, read a
marriage enhancement book together or
attend a marriage class or seminar. He'll love
it if you make all the arrangements.

106

All wives offend their husbands at some point. Some
are oblivious to their husband's hurt, some ignore it,
and some admit their offense and ask forgiveness.
What has been your pattern? Practice asking
forgiveness. It will draw you closer together.

107

On a scale of 0 to 10, where would you rate your marriage today? Where would your husband rate it? Predict his answer and then ask him.

108

Remember that love isn't an act; it's a way of life. It's being there during good times and not-so-good times. Being there is always possible when Jesus is invited to be there, too.

109
Does the TV in your home build your marriage relationship or detract from it? Ask your husband if he
would agree to keep the television off for a
month so you can work on your
communication with each other.

110

Marriage often turns out to be more than you expected. But you and your husband can shape the future of your marriage by determining its direction. List three common goals you and your husband have for your marriage. If you don't have any, don't wait any longer!

111

Make it your business to know at least five of your
husband's needs and how to meet those needs
in a way he desires. Most men, for example,
have a need for admiration. It would be
difficult to give too many compliments!

112
The marriage relationship is God's way of reflecting his eternal love for his people. What priority should we give to it? What priority do you give to it?

113
Listen for God's voice. "And if you leave God's paths and go astray, you will hear a Voice behind you say, 'No, this way; walk here'" (Isaiah 30:21 LB).

114

God does not quit on us. A wife's wedding vows to
her husband are a reflection of God's pledge to never
leave us and never give up on us. What area of your
marriage could use more attention and effort?

115
Have you ever thought about what your husband
might look like twenty years from now, or
what you might look like? Talk with him
about your thoughts.

116
Be careful what you say to your husband in anger.
Never say anything that reflects on his abilities or
diminishes who he is as a person. Hurt that comes
from angry words can last long after you've forgotten
what your anger was all about.

117

Men are quite sensitive to criticism. Think positive:
give your husband suggestions and time to think
about them rather than a negative "Why did you
do that?" or "I know a better way to do it."

118

Being your husband's friend means encouraging him
to reach his potential and delighting in his success
as if you had just won the Miss America contest.
Think of a personal goal your husband has
recently achieved and plan a celebration
with a few close friends.

119

Change is a vital part of a growing marriage. List three
ways you are different this year compared to last. Ask
your husband what he thinks.

120

Think of two or three recent times you've shared with
your husband feelings of failure, sadness, or
disappointment. If you can't, today's a
new day. Let him see you as you are.

121

Make a list of your needs and ask God to show you
which are important. Let Him decide. Better to lead
a God-centered life than a need-centered life.

122

Forgiveness in marriage is tied to grace rather than
justice. It lets your husband off the hook. It doesn't
make him pay again and again for the same
failure. Forgive and forget.

123
Failing doesn't make you a failure in your
marriage. Giving up, withdrawing, viewing
yourself as a failure, and refusing to learn
from your experience might!

124
Tell your husband that he's more important to
you than work or household tasks—then
find some way to prove it to him!

125

Friendship between a husband and wife is rated as the
number one reason for marital happiness. Having a
close friendship comes from *being* a good friend.
Laughing, playing, talking, and working
together builds friendship.

126
"The more important a man feels he is to his wife,
the more he encourages her to do the
activities he knows she enjoys."[11]

127

On a scale of 0 to 10, how important are your
possessions to you? "Then [Jesus] said to them,
'Watch out! Be on your guard against all
kinds of greed; a man's life does not
consist in the abundance of his possessions'"
(Luke 12:15 NIV).

128
Remember you don't need to look for guidance in the
areas where God has already said "Yes" and has
given a command. All you need is to be obedient.[12]
Should you love your husband?
No question!

129

When a woman loves her husband, she opens herself up to a new level of hurt. But understand that when a man doesn't feel loved or respected by his wife, the pain of rejection is intense. Take the risk. Tell your husband daily that you love and appreciate him.

130

The next time you are sick, notice how you act with
your husband. Are you pleasant or unapproachable?
Are you easy to take care of or should you be
confined to an isolation ward?! Your husband
may be able to tell you.

131

A wife doesn't *have* to submit to her husband, care for
him, help him. She *gets* to! Tell your husband you've
learned it's a privilege to love him. Ask how
you can help him even more.

132

"The only time to stop temptation is at the point of
recognition. If one begins to argue and engage in
a hand-to-hand combat, temptation almost
always wins the day."[13]

133

Women often relate to God in one of four ways: "Give me," "Use me," "Make me," or "Search me, O God, and know my heart." Where are you today?

134

Don't let the sun go down on your anger.
Resolve your differences as soon as possible—
a great idea in marriage.

135

A 50/50 marriage doesn't work; it's too hard
to figure out if you and your husband have
both come halfway. With a 100/100
commitment, there isn't a question.

136

Tell your husband how you see God working in your
lives. "Unless the Lord builds the house, its builders
labor in vain" (Psalm 127:1 NIV).

137
Remind yourself often that wives who give a little
love find it goes a long way, and wives who give
a lot of love find it just keeps going and
going and going forever.

138
Tell your husband on a regular basis, "I love you more
than yesterday and less than tomorrow."

139
Write your husband a note telling him he's a
memorable person and why.[14]

140

The next time you find yourself arguing with
your husband, ask yourself, "Is my goal to
punish and dominate my husband, or
to understand him?" If needed, redirect
your arguments toward the
goal of reconciliation.

141

Romance is like a coal that needs your breath
and patience to ignite. If you want a stronger
marriage, take a few breaths and blow!

142
Your husband has a love bank. Every time you interact
with him you make a deposit or a withdrawal.
Have you checked the ledger lately?
Keep those books balanced![15]

143

When a wife gives her husband second place—because
she gives her work, children, or some other interest
first place—he has three choices. He can accept second
place, press for first place and eventually win, or
press for first place until he loses heart.
Why put him through that?[16]

144
Ask your husband how the way you handle frustration
or express anger makes him feel and how it affects
your marriage. Do you draw him closer or
push him away? Ask him how you could
express those feelings differently.

145

A quality wife is one who can satisfy one man all her life long—and who can be satisfied by one man all her life long. It takes effort, time, commitment, and the grace of God, but it's possible. Make this your goal for the life of your marriage.

146

If your marriage seems dull, perhaps it's you! Maybe
you're stuck in your routine. Maybe you're too
predictable. Shock your husband! Be unusually
creative and totally unpredictable. Fix him
new meals, dress differently, sit on his lap....

147

If it takes time for you to recover from a quarrel
with your husband, that's all right. Healing can't
be rushed. But remember that his sense of timing
is different from your own. If he seems to
recover more quickly than you, it doesn't
mean he's insensitive or he didn't really
care about the issue. Give him the
benefit of the doubt.

148

"Instead of focusing on our mates—how much is
lacking—let's look at ourselves and the size of the
debt God has forgiven us. Surely He bears
with our failings. Let us commit to bear
with each other's failings when we are
weak and build each other up."[17]

149
Think about the time you spend working, whether at home or in a job setting. Tell your husband what your work means to you and what you would like to be doing in your work ten years from now.

150

Talk with your husband on an ongoing basis about
how both you and he would like your marriage to
be different. Listen without defensiveness. Take
time out to think about his ideas and yours,
and come back to the discussion later.

151

So you're on your way somewhere and your husband
is lost! Instead of pointing it out and demanding that
he stop for directions, try one of these alternatives:
"What do you want to do?" "Can I do something
to help?" "I don't mind being late. Want to
make this a wild adventure?!"

152

When your husband walks in the door after work, how
is he greeted? To what do you give your immediate
attention? Your husband wants to be Number One.
Before you do anything else, greet him with
affection and genuine interest: "I've missed you,"
"It's good to see you," "Tell me about your day."
Don't hit him with problems, negatives, or
"Do you know what *your* kids did today?!"
until he's had a chance to unwind.

153

A husband and wife who are friends don't attempt to control or dominate one another. Respect your husband's ideas and feelings. Ask often, "What do you think?" Say often, "Let's try it your way."

154

The love-talk that a couple shares before marriage is too often, after marriage, replaced by other kinds of communication. Take time to reflect, then list the things you used to talk about. Ask your husband to do the same. Introduce those topics back into your conversations.

155

Encourage your husband in specific ways. A man who
knows his wife supports him will trust her more
and be more open.

156

Talking may not be everything, but it sure beats avoiding important issues. Avoidance causes problems to
grow. When you find yourself avoiding your husband,
ask yourself, "What is our disagreement?
How can we resolve it?"

157

Conflict can open as many doors as it closes in a
marriage. When you allow it to open a door between
you and your husband, you'll see your differences
disappear. What are some things you can do to
resolve some of your differences? Think about
it and come up with a list of ideas.

158
Ask your husband how you could be better at loving
and serving him. Be ready to hear his answer.
Thank him for his suggestions.

159
Love in marriage says, "Will you forgive me for the
hurt I've caused you?" When have you said this?
Do you need to say it now?

160
When a husband and wife talk about their thoughts
and feelings with each other, every problem is
diminished and every joy expanded. Share
often, but for best results, be brief.

161

"Sex is a God-ordained means of assuring your partner that he is the most important person in the world right here, right now." Make it creative, romantic, and sensitive to your husband's needs and timing.[18]

162
When your husband left for work this morning,
did he feel supported and built up by
having been home? Ask!

163
Lines open to God are invariably open to one another,
for a woman cannot be genuinely open to God
and closed to her mate.[19]

164
When you love and support the best in your husband,
many of the things that irritate you either disappear
or don't bother you as much.

165

When you find yourself arguing with your husband,
stop yourself and listen to him. Then respond with,
"If I understand your position, you are saying..."
and restate what you heard. When you stop to
consider both sides of an issue, you'll be
amazed how marital discord diminishes.

166

When your husband has had a bad day, the best words
you can say are, "I believe in you, and so does God.
What can I do to make the rest of your day easier?"

167

Who hears about it when you're upset with your husband? Nobody? Your mother? Your friends? Next time, let him know directly but calmly that you are upset, what you would like him to do differently, and that you know he is capable of it.

168
Farm out the kids and have a romantic interlude in the
living room or family room. He'll love it!

169
When your husband is struggling with a problem,
ask if he wants suggestions before giving them.
If he does, give them gently and lovingly.
Be aware of your tone of voice.

170

Go to the library and check out a book of romantic poems. Ask your husband to select one and read it to you just before bedtime some evening.

171

Sex and verbal communication cannot be separated. One is not a substitute for the other. But remember that for most men sex is a form of communication. Lovemaking helps your husband feel accepted.

172
Scripture teaches us to praise God (Psalm 100:4) and
others (Ephesians 4:29). Think of three ways
you've praised your husband recently.

173
Keep in mind that love is concern for what concerns
your husband. If he doesn't tell you what his concerns
are, make up a list of twenty or thirty common concerns and ask him to check off several.

174
A hug or caress along with your words will make your
husband feel more understood and accepted,
especially when he's tired.

175
Come up with a list of gifts you *think* your husband
would like to receive from you. Show him the list
and ask his opinion. How well did you do?
Give him one of his choices this week.

176

Want your husband to make some kind of change?
He'll be more open if the change makes sense to
him, he doesn't feel blamed for not doing it
right, he finds that it works, and he
receives reinforcement for it from you.[20]

177

If you think of your husband as uncommunicative, try
thinking of him as precise and to the point instead.
Learn something new from his directness
and ability to condense!

178

Marriage is the best place to alter bad habits or offensive behaviors. Has your husband ever mentioned any to you? Ask him if there's anything you do he would prefer you didn't do.

179

Instead of criticizing your husband for leaving his clothes on the floor, thank him when he remembers to hang them up.

180
Be patient before God when the road seems long.
"But those who wait on the Lord shall renew their
strength; they shall mount up with wings like eagles,
they shall run and not be weary. They shall walk
and not faint" (Isaiah 40:31 NKJV).

181

Feeling trapped? When everyone in your life is demanding a piece of you and there isn't enough to go around, slip away for a quiet conversation with someone you know will just listen. How about God?

182
If your work, abilities, or attractiveness were taken
away from you for the next six months, how
would you feel about yourself? Discuss this
question with your husband sometime.

183

"A generous man will prosper; he who refreshes others
will himself be refreshed" (Proverbs 11:25 NIV). List
the ways that you are generous toward your husband.
Time? Housework? Money? How else?

184
Would you like to discover the will of God for your marriage? Go before God together. Ask Him what He wants for your marriage and determine to do it!

185
"If we wait until we have resolved every doubt, every question, before following God, we will never do anything with our life. We must step out by faith."[21]

186
Be conscious of your prayer requests. Are your
prayers compatible with the character of God
or would He violate His nature by giving
you what you're asking for?[22]

187
Develop an early warning system to combat temptation in your life. Pray together with your husband
every day. Memorize 1 Corinthians 10:13 together.

188
How does your husband know that you really care for
him? List three specific ways. If you don't know, ask.
Then ask, "How else would you like to be cared for?"

189

Talk to your husband *when* you're upset, not after the fact. Spell it out for him. He may not be as intuitive as you are, and he certainly can't read your mind!

190

In one of your braver moments, ask your husband for three things you could improve on. Tell him you respect his judgment and you'd like his help in becoming a better wife.

191

Give your husband permission to say "No" when you ask for his help or support. He'll be more open to responding to your next request.[23]

192

Love can die when a husband and wife forget how to talk to each other, when they don't make time for romance.[24] Surprise your husband this week with a romantic evening you plan yourself.

193

Write your husband a note that says, "You just go on getting better every day!"[25] Tape it to the mirror in the bathroom.

194

The best way to tell your husband about something you don't like is to tell him about something you *do* like. For example: "I really appreciate it when you call to tell me you're going to be late."

195

"When our mates have strengths we should affirm them, but never pressure them to perform. To criticize our mates at the point of their strength is to kill their courage."[26]

196

Are you pressuring your husband to spend more time at work to make more money? Think about having him spend that time with the family instead. You may not accumulate as many things, but investing in lives pays great dividends.

197
An inexpensive gift that gives a thousand percent
return is an activities calendar with "Special Husband
Time" written on several days of each month.

198
Talk to your husband about his thoughts and concerns
about your marriage. Learn to see life through his eyes
as well as your own. He may see things you miss.

199

Some wives fail to contribute to their husband's happiness, some actively contribute to his unhappiness, and some make him feel like the most important man on earth. How does your husband feel?

200

Take your husband away for a romantic weekend. Tell him in advance you will not think or talk about projects at home or the kids, you won't discuss problems, and you won't hide your nose in a book. Be his servant for the weekend.

201

Reflect on the ways you communicated with your husband in the early days of your courtship. How did two strangers become intimate friends? Did you discuss dreams, goals, your faith, hobbies? Think of three ways you communicate with him now that keeps your intimacy alive. If you can't, ask him for feedback.

202
Don't assume you know what your husband is going to say before he says it. Assumptions lead to distortions, so listen carefully. He may surprise you!

203
Forgive truly. "Forgiving" your husband only if he promises never to fail again is not forgiveness. True forgiveness trusts and believes in the one you love.

204

Overlook your husband's shortcomings, but never overlook his potential! Let him know you believe in him. Ask how you can help him reach his goals.[27]

205

Husbands and wives comfort one another in time of need. How does your husband like you to comfort him? Don't guess about this—ask if you don't know. How do you prefer him to comfort you? Tell him.

206
Teach your husband gently. Use positive modeling,
gentle prodding, encouraging words.
Let him know you believe in him.

207
Be teachable. Listen to your husband, learn from his
positive modeling, accept his gentle prodding.
He believes in you!

208

If you haven't already, you will experience the death of
a parent, a close friend, a child, or your spouse. Now is
the time to think about how you will handle it.
Talk with your husband about it.

209

Your husband married you because he believed the
wonderful, attentive way you responded to him in
courtship would continue and increase after marriage.
Is that kind of response still there and growing,
or do you need to recommit?

210

Give your husband permission to grumble when you ask him to do something for you. Grumbling means he's considering your request—better than an outright "No!" Give him time. It's okay.[28]

211

When you bring up a problem or concern with your husband, tell him the bottom line first. He will be more apt to hear the rest of the details.

212
Whenever you think, "I should have listened to him,"
let your husband know. He will appreciate your
acknowledgment that he was right.

213
Tape-record a week's worth of family dinner conversations. When you play back the tape, listen to your tone
of voice. What are you communicating that you didn't
realize you were? Concentrate on *how* you say things
as well as what you say.

214

Recognize that the responsibility of the marriage is not yours alone and behave accordingly. Share the responsibility with your husband, and let him know you are sharing it. Ask him to plan six special dates for the year. Tell him you'd be thrilled if he would select a book on communication or sex and read it to you.

215

Be a sensitive listener. Give your husband feedback to let him know you're listening, but avoid interrupting or correcting him.

216

Ask your husband which of your emotional responses
he has the most difficulty accepting. Ask how he
would prefer you to respond, thank him for the
suggestion, and consider what he has to say.

217

If your husband uses a day-by-day calendar, "borrow"
it to write a personal message of love on the first
and fifteenth of each month.

218
In your marital disagreements, do you take the role of
solution-finder or fault-finder? Only one role allows
both you and your husband to be winners.
Fixing blame isn't it!

219
Listen to your husband. Sit down, stop what you're
doing, and really *listen*. It's the only way to
find out what's important to him.

220
Things aren't working the way you want them to in your marriage? Identify what you need, relate it to your husband's interests, and share a little at a time to keep his curiosity stimulated.[29]

221
"Marriage is not so much finding the right person as it is *being* the right person."[30] Are you the wife you wanted to be when you married? If not, it's still possible to become that woman.

222

Show your husband you appreciate both the big and
little things he does for you. Otherwise
he might feel discouraged.

NOTES

1. John Gray, *Men Are from Mars and Women Are from Venus* (New York: Harper Collins, 1992), 253, adapted.

2. Gray, 135, adapted.

3. John Gray, *What Your Mother Didn't Tell You and Your Father Didn't Know* (New York: Harper Collins, 1994), 157, adapted.

4. Paul Tournier, *The Healing of Persons* (New York: Harper and Row, 1965), 88-89.

5. Gray, *What Your Mother Didn't Tell You and Your Father Didn't Know,* 164, adapted.

6. Gary Smalley, *For Better or For Best* (Grand Rapids, Mich.: Zondervan, 1979), 75, adapted.

7. David Wilkerson, *I'm Not Mad at God* (Minneapolis: Bethany Fellowship, 1967), 32.

8. Charlie Shedd, *Letters to Philip* (Old Tappan, N.J.: Revell, 1968), 64.

9. James R. Bjorge, *Forty Ways to Say I Love You* (Minneapolis: Augsburg, 1978), 59-60.

10. Bjorge, 24.

11. Smalley, 47.

12. A.W. Tozer. Adapted, source unknown.

13. Thomas à Kempis.

14. Shedd, 31.

15. Willard F. Harley, Jr. *His Needs, Her Needs* (Grand Rapids, Mich.: Revell, 1986), 13.

16. Patrick M. Morley, *Two Part Harmony* (Nashville: Nelson, 1994), 79, adapted.

17. Morley, 143.

18. Charlie Shedd, *Letters to Karen* (Nashville: Abingdon, 1965), 111.

19. Dwight Small, *After You Say I Do* (Grand Rapids, Mich.: Revell, 1968), 214.

20. Gray, *What Your Mother Didn't Tell You and Your Father Didn't Know,* 263, adapted.

21. Richard Exley, *The Making of a Man* (Tulsa, Okla: Honor, 1993), 141.

22. Exley, 173, adapted.

23. Gray, *Men Are from Mars and Women Are from Venus,* 264, adapted.

24. James Dobson, *Dr. Dobson Answers Your Questions* (Wheaton, Ill.: Tyndale, 1982), 329.

25. Shedd, *Letters to Philip,* 33.

26. Morley, 143.

27. Bjorge, 30, adapted.

28. Gray, *Men Are from Mars and Women Are from Venus,* 266, adapted.

29. Smalley, 48.

30. Shedd, *Letters to Karen,* 13.